For Jean —
affectionately,
Celeste

16 May 1974

A SENSE OF PLACE

Also by Celeste Turner Wright:

Etruscan Princess and Other Poems

A Sense of Place

by

CELESTE TURNER WRIGHT

THE GOLDEN QUILL PRESS
Publishers
Francestown　　　　New Hampshire

Library of Congress Catalog Card Number 73-86533

ISBN 8233-0196-6

Printed in the United States of America

To Howard Baker and Bob Wiggins,

who have also labored on this book

FOREWORD

"State of Preservation" received the Reynolds Lyric Award for 1963. Both "The Jewel-Box at Bradford" and "Minor Medici" won Grand Prizes in the annual Ina Coolbrith Circle competitions (open to all California poets).

Years of composition appear under *Contents*. Certain poems have been much revised since their first printing.

Not reprinted here are the thirty-six poems in my *Etruscan Princess* (Alan Swallow, Denver, 1964). Also omitted—sometimes for lack of space, sometimes because of maternal rejection—are fifty-six poems that have been in magazines, besides half-a-dozen that the Pasadena *Star-News* charitably adopted when I was a freshman at UCLA.

For permission to reprint seventy-two of the seventy-three poems here collected, I thank *Alentour, The American Bard, The American Poet, American Weave, The Archer, The Arizona Quarterly, The Beloit Poetry Journal, Cimarron Review, Different, Down East, Essence, The Florida Magazine of Verse, Imprints Quarterly, Kaleidograph, The Laurel Review* (and *The New Laurel Review*), *The Lyric, Maelstrom, Midwestern University Quarterly, Modern American Lyrics, Poet Lore, The Poetry Chapbook, Poetry Newsletter, Poetry Venture, Prairie Poet, Prairie Schooner, Queen's Quarterly* (Canada), *Quoin, South and West, The Southern Poetry Review, The University Review, Verse Craft, Voices, The West Coast Review* (Canada), *Westward,* and *Wings*.

CONTENTS

A SENSE OF PLACE

THE ABBOT'S KITCHEN
Glastonbury, England

A mirror once safeguarded contemplation
Of gorgons who could stare a man to stone,
But this one saves your neck from dislocation
While you survey the kitchen roof, a cone.
Astronomers entrap a constellation
In mirrors, but this glass reflects your own
Mundanest features in a transformation—
They seem to dangle loosely from the bone.

Thus bending like a mortified Narcissus,
You gaze and marvel at the acrobat
Ceiling that climbs as though it were ambitious
To be a steeple or a witch's hat.
 This was the hangout of the abbot's bakers,
 Used later as a meeting-house for Quakers.

AGAINST MAILING A LETTER

Stretch but this anther of your feeling forth
And it may generate a growing need,
Till you, despite benevolence and worth,
Will shrink from the emotion that you breed.
Unlooked-for, sisterlike, your eloquence
May bring her disappointment, vainly stir
A hope of taking comfort in such friends:
You sympathize; you are not drawn to her.

Silence is better than this fervency
From sources even to yourself unknown—
An indiscriminate humanity
Or some embosomed grievance of your own.
    May God forgive us, not for sharing pain
    But showing love we cannot long sustain.

THE ARRAIGNMENT

"Here on my knees find safe repose,"
  Sang Beauty to the Strongest One.
(Shear him and open to his foes!)
  Lady, was this well done?

"Welcome from Troy," another said;
  "Anew our marriage is begun."
Under her net his bath ran red.
  Lady, was this well done?

Gallant to grapple enemies
  As a relentless champion,
But to work furtively like these—
  Lady, was this well done?

Gallant to smite the foe in view,
  Like a barbaric amazon;
But he who loved and trusted you—
  Lady, was this well done?

THE ARTIFICIAL FIREPLACE

"There is no heartbeat in our house," said she;
    There was no hearth; they'd scanted in the plan.
Two autumns later he remorsefully
    Sent home a fireplace complete by van.

With it came bellows—genuine, for show—
    Andirons also. When she snapped a switch,
Shadows would flicker, a convincing glow
    Throbbed from the applewood within the niche.

She thanked him: "Dear, how thoughtful!" she would say.
    But sitting by it on the ottoman,
She shivered on a warm September day
    And wondered when the counterfeit began.

ASTRONAUT

Floating within a satellite, Mankind
For the first time impartially has watched
Our world—a heartsick painter studying
Afar the canvas he has blindly botched.

He sees the warring continents outspread
And jagged, like a puzzle wrenched apart,
Unreconciled as his frustrated will
To the vagaries of a neighbor's heart.

Yet if that spaceship were a paradise
Where he might glide immortal, he would yearn
For his outrageous brothers and drop tears
By Earthlight, wishing only to return.

17

AT HARDSCRABBLE
Mount Kineo, Maine

The mountain turned its back upon that place;
To her it was the dark side of the moon;
Yet she came seeking the abandoned farm.
The little girl saw in the clearing there
A shack, a gray futility of barn,
Where hunters tore off boards to make their fires.

The woods were silent. She reflected how
Rarely a steamboat whistle echoing
Startled the hollow cliffside; once a year
The ragged mane of icicles that hung
All winter from the mountain broke away
And thundered down into a hidden valley.

Red-fruited brambles nodded near the barn,
Nippled with raspberries that disengaged
Their warmth and sweetness at her fingertips.
She feasted in security until
A grain of torment agonized her tongue—
The ant Formica, stinging from the fruit.

Later she found the cabin door ajar
And glimpsed a broken stove, a bunk with boughs
Where something grunted, something bristled up
Like long dry needles of the evergreen—
An angry porcupine, and she supposed
That he could dart his arrows at her eyes.

Outside again, she rallied to her plan
For conquering the mountaintop alone.
Up near the summit she and Father once
Drank from the common dipper at a spring;
Then, standing where the airy bluebells waved
On random earth the flint had pocketed,
They gazed across the whitecaps of the lake,
Moose River veining through some pastureland,
And the infinity of northern pines.
She would regain that vision by herself,
Triumphantly courageous—though a child.

The upward trail was unmistakable;
But after she had labored forty yards,
Terror curtailed her breathing, stopped her climb.
Across the pathway, motionless, a snake
Lay staring at her with its whitish eyes.
Was it a presence or an empty skin?
She could not look, for rivulets of ice
Trickled throughout her body. Though her pride
Faintly suggested, *Climb another way*,
The loosened rocks appeared precarious,
And her unruly legs were hurrying
Downhill already, waiting no command.

Down she was plunging, routed, unashamed,
Homeward to childishness, dependency,
Running with painful stitches in her side.

AT THE FAIRGROUNDS
San Francisco

Only the toiling pumps had won
   The palm roots respite from the zone
Of salt; reality was none
   In that synthetic heaven; the drone
   Of Strauss came from a microphone;
But readily we paid the price
   And paced to music of our own
   In our September paradise.

We knew the island was begun
   From rocks that clever men had strown
Upon the Bay, a skeleton
   Artfully fleshed, manured, and sown
   With grass; but garden plots had grown
In starred or circular device,
   And summer roses were full-blown
   In our September paradise.

The plaster Tower of the Sun
   Was soaring like immortal stone,
And when they played the carillon,
   With ocean sunsets in the tone,
   A sweetness balmed the very bone,
As of a mummy lapt in spice.
   Heart groped for heart; we dreamed alone
   In our September paradise.

Long since, the tower is overthrown;
There are no fountains to entice;

The tatters of the fog are blown
In our September paradise.

BRICK FACADE
Florence

Despite the beauty of the church within,
The front of San Lorenzo's looks forlorn,
With bricks as ragged as if thieves by night
Had stripped away some precious ornament.
Viewed from afar, the wall resembles clay,
Mud tablets of the Babylonians,
To be imprinted with a human thought.

That message should be Michelangelo's;
He promised a harmonious facade:
Pilasters, marble statues, bas-reliefs,
To dazzle Florence and all Italy.

The wall remains unsightly, featureless.
Why did it never waken to his hand,
As, in the miracle he painted once,
The clay of Adam greets God's fingertips?

He worked as if the rhythm in his veins
Assured him that his span was ninety years.
Exulting, he had offered to the Pope
More wonders than a giant could perform;
Then, overburdened, laid aside his art.

He went perversely to seek quarries out
Himself, and engineered a mountain road;
But when the river, shallow in the heat,
No longer floated heavy barges down,
He would not touch the marble he had stored.

After five years, the Medici gave up,
Slighted their parish church; but greater blame
Devolved on him for squandering his prime.
When he was ninety, and the city knelt
At San Lorenzo's for his requiem,
Some pictured how his spirit, near those bricks,
Must rue the idling of such talents there—
"The sin," they said, "against the Holy Ghost!"

BRIEF COMMUNION

Dear love, I waited for our sacrament,
   But went away as hungry as before:
Preoccupied, my priest had spilled the wine
   And almost dropped the wafer on the floor.

BUCKEYE HONEY: A FABLE
California

The laboring unselfish bee
That summer month she is alive
Makes half a golden teaspoonful
Of contribution to her hive.

Along the hills today I saw
Poisonous honey-plants delude
Bee nations into storing up
Death for themselves and for their brood.

DINNER TIME AT PORT ROYAL
Jamaica, 7 June 1692

Noon was an hour of security,
Good humor, with a beef-and-turtle stew
In Jemmy's cookhouse; there the long clay pipes
And onion-shaped Madeira bottles danced,
Pulsating as a bosun roared his jokes,
The saltier for wenches' tittering.

Siesta time would follow, curtained well
From the Jamaican sun and pillowed soft
On the assurance of prosperity:
Cotton, tobacco, rum, and sugar stacked
Up to the rafters of the warehouse roof.

O thriving city, once the waterfront
Most harborsome to Henry Morgan's mates;
Port Royal—marketplace, emporium,
Lusty Gomorrah of the Caribbean!

"Twenty to noontime," registered the tick
Of Captain Williams' watch from Amsterdam;
Warm in his pocket and invisible,
It promised dinner: "Twenty minutes to."

Earth heaved and shook like billows; earthy mouths
Opened to swallow men; the houses cracked;
The tall brick buildings on that sandy spit
Dissolved in ocean like so many cubes
Of sugar in a bowl of planter's punch.

For centuries the soupbones in their pot
Lay under silting of the harbor floor,
Beside a lantern and a candlestick.
Down there the sherry, though securely corked,
Became the bitterest Golgothan brew,
And coral thickened on the shining brass
Of Williams' treasure. (Water-scorpions
And barracuda never ask the time.)
When divers finally salvaged it, they found
The hands affirming, "Eighteen minutes to."

DISTRUST

How did it enter? Lousemeal, rat by rat,
Stealing along a hawser from the town;
The hold was balmy with an Eastern freight
Until the scabrous pelts came smirching down.

Only a patter, slight the evil; then
Profound contamination. Though the sun
Burnished her name, in the forgotten gloom
Below the waterline the barque was foul,
Vermined with doubts and feverish with doom.

THE DRY HARBOR
Miletus

Here lies the harbor; on the nettled soil
Launch, if you can, your boat!   The olive trees
Enshadow ancient seawall; bumblebees
Drone and the lazy leopard-snakes uncoil
Where quinqueremes disburdened of their spoil
Once lifted foamy bosoms, and the breeze
Astray from Chios over purple seas
Freshened the rower's forehead after toil.

A thousand years this barren spot has lain
Many miles inland; but the surge shall fall
Exultant on these cliffs and sweep the plain,
The galley's beak shall drink, the helmsman call,
Sooner than buoyancy and health again
May overflow the world beyond this wall.

DUMDO
East Holden, Maine

After the red-haired sow had farrowed,
She overlay three tiny brothers;
Grandfather said how treacherous
Great Solomon had found such mothers.
I helped him build a nursery,
Warmed by a lightbulb, to protect
My sleeping Dumdo and the others.

Dumdo was not a common pig:
He had a winsome pointed face
And stepped on tiptoe daintily—
Oh, how unlike his mother's pace!
His barn might smell of sour milk,
But there I spent my breathing space;
Despite the garbage and the squeals,
A hogpen was a lovely place.

Next year, while I was visiting,
A butcher knocked upon the door,
A cauldron boiled beside the barn.
I stumbled to the second floor,
But even underneath my bed
I heard the hideous uproar—
Three Little Pigs reversed—and since
Grandfather had become the Wolf,
I did not love him any more.

FAMILY PHOTOGRAPH
Riverside, California

The couple came from Tennessee
Early and bought an orange grove;
Hovered like parents round each tree
Until at last the venture throve.

But long before the fight was won,
Those two were weary, searched with pain;
The photograph they left their son
Reveals them awkward, gaunt, and plain.

When rich men want an ancestor,
Brushes can soften the uncouth;
Art will retouch the ragged hair,
Blot galluses, and mend a tooth.

In meretricious dignity
There stands the product on the shelf,
Deceptive as biography
Or a man's image of himself.

FLAGELLATE

Always too tentative to leave a trace,
Yet everlasting. First a commonplace
Speck that the random water might suspend.
Then the vitality the sun begot
Or lightning quickened—a parental dot,
Selfless in subdivision without end.

Eternities thereafter some decree
Magnetized into personality
A cluster that had once been meaningless;
And thus with the announcement, "I am here,"
That glob of jelly, flagellated sphere,
Chose death, the penalty for separateness.

GRAPEVINE

Intruders, muscat leaves, were peeping through
My oriental tree's exotic fans:
A few transparent spirals, like sweet peas
Or like the fingers of a baby who
Clings for a moment to his mother's hands.
But when I twitched a tendril, I could see
Great shudders passing through the gingko tree.

Grapes are not orchids, cannot feed on air;
Unnoticed hitherto, a wooden stem,
Scaly and thick, was crawling up the trunk
And forking through the branches; in a month,
Like pride or jealousy pervading men,
The grapevine would be strangling the top,
Reducing all that beauty to a prop.

Removal of the younger shoots would not
Preserve the gingko long from insolence;
I took a saw and furiously cut
Into the rootstock swagging off the fence;
Gritting my teeth, I gashed it anywise,
With gnats and sawdust burning in my eyes.

The cut went deeper as I dogged the work;
The root divided with a sudden crack;
Like any peasant harnessed to a plow,
I hauled that tangle loose behind my back.
The ground was hummocky, my hands were sore,
But when those hateful ropes came trailing free,
I was a giant who bestrode the sea
Towing a hundred captured men-of-war.

GUIDE AT MOOSEHEAD LAKE
Maine

Her stool with deerfeet had been named for him;
It was his present, and she called it Jim.
Stroking the polished hooves, the soft brown hair
Over its ankles, she recalled her fear
And rapture when he used to hold her high
To pat a moosehead, poke its glassy eye,
Explore the antlers—giant fingers, clawed.

Jim was a French Canadian, a god.
He shot the rapids as Penobscots do.
Once when she crossed the lake in his canoe
A squall upheaved the whitecaps; Mother prayed—
But in such keeping, who could be afraid!

Adventuring along the wharf, she found
A swollen burlap bag upon the ground
And hungered, knowing that this gunny sack
Brought bread for the Italians at the shack,
The railroad workers. Overtempted, she
Raveled the corner stitches lawlessly,
Ate half a loaf extracted from the bag,
Then smuggled the remainder of her swag
Into the stable, to the harness room,
Where Jim was helping sometimes as a groom.
He hid it in a closet he would guard,
But she forgot until the loaf was hard.
Then how his moustache laughed! He stroked her head:
"When you are big, I'll marry you," he said.

He jilted her the summer she was eight.
Her relatives were camping by the lake,
On Sugar Island, thick with evergreens.
One day as she was sharing their baked beans
And cucumbers, a light canoe slipped in
With Jimmy steering. Jealousy, chagrin
Checked her excitement when he came ashore:
He did not recognize her any more;
Beside him walked a pretty girl, who sped
Into the forest with averted head.

There was a tent concealed among the pines;
A cousin showed her where at suppertime
And whispered, "They've been coming all along;
Since they're not married, naturally it's wrong."
She little cared about iniquity;
She only thought, "He never looked at me."

Jim took that woman for his wife, and need
Drove him next winter to a fearful deed:
He entered freight cars, breaking seals as well,
And took illegal whiskey off to sell.
The child stole bread; unlucky Jim was caught
And punished for a theft, but she was not.

In June her mother with a woman friend
Went touring through a prison and was pained
To find Jim suffering for his mishap
Like one of his own foxes in a trap.
He glimpsed the visitors through bars that day,
Then turned his handsome head and looked away.

HANDSOME UNKNOWN

Sir, it was not indifference made me hurry
    After I glimpsed you in the marketplace;
Sweet was the shock, tumultuous the flurry
    Stirred in my woman's heart by such a face.

But you are human, and I've learned the sequels:
    Smiling the selfish, exquisite and hollow!
Lessons like these were taught me by your equals:
    Charming, the faunlike face—till goatlegs follow.

Since this is true, O Stranger, and I know it,
    Locked in my room a solid hour I've sat
Loving the gentleman, the knight, the poet
    You should have been with such a face as that.

THE HOUSE THAT ISN'T THERE
New Place, Stratford-on-Avon

Thanks to Mr. Francis Gastrell,
A divine of frightful temper,
The forlornest place in Stratford
Is the house that isn't there.

Thanks to him, we cannot view it,
Varnished like a Stradivarius,
Full of joint-stools never Shakespeare's
But "all dating from his time."

No one shows the bed "reputed
To have been his second-best one,"
Nor the inglenook where Jonson
And the Bard "may well have sipped."

Lackaday! The Reverend Francis
Bought the Place, but in a fury
Over taxes tore the house down
(Seventeen and Fifty-nine).

Wellaway!—though grief is lessened
When we learn that other owners
Had rebuilt from scratch to thatches
Only fifty years before.

Just the well remains—authentic,
Or at least I like to think so;
I am one with Shakespeare, staring
Downward at those very stones.

It is round as Falstaff's belly,
Deeper than Mercutio's death-wound;
Even for King Richard's kingdom,
Horses cannot pull it up.

ICY HARVEST
Maine

To fill the storehouse on the bank a crew
Were sawing channels in the frozen lake
And pushing heavy blocks that bobbed along;
The ice-crop, mealed with sawdust, garnered up,
Would freshen summer at the great hotel.
Old Amos gave the child a pointed pole
And let her work an hour at his side;
The sunshine twinkled on the floating ice.

But later, when she skimmed away on skates
To see the woodsmen hauling logs across,
She found them clustered where a team had drowned:
Two giant horses, plunging through the ice,
Strapped to their loaded sledge, had buffeted
Until their hearts came to a stony stop.
The bodies, sodden from the water, lay
Enormous on the ice-road, glazing stiff,
With desperation frozen in their eyes.
Thick tongues protruded; icicles encroached
On mouths that often, warm and velvety,
Had lipped the sugar from her proffered palm.

Delight was murdered, for the glassy miles
Revealed this other possibility;
Terror now gaped where she had moved secure
In the deceitful glitter of the sun.

IN THE REPAIR SHOP

"When Mother was alive this clock would function,
But now it registers by fits and starts;
She used to soothe it with a little unction—
Patience and coaxing for the stubborn parts.

"Sundials last whole generations longer:
Shadows on marble cause no wear and tear.
Since complicated things are never stronger,
These works will be the mischief to repair.

"It mutters like a parrot going crazy.
Perhaps the balance wheel has come unhooked?
Don't smile because my speculation's hazy,
But give your diagnosis when you've looked."

"Sorry, my tinkering won't make it better;
As you can see, its hands will hardly stir.
The firm is still in business; write a letter
And send this to the manufacturer."

IN THOSE DAYS
Berkeley, California

Do you remember August in the hills—
The cobwebs floating and the thistle seed,
The dandelion fluff . . . that lazy hawk
Watching the rabbit in the sunburnt weed?

We were as windblown as the rest,
Emancipate as they,
Dancing upon a filament
Over the hills and bay.

THE JEWEL-BOX AT BRADFORD
England

A queen once dreamed about the buried Cross;
The saint who taught our Wessex towns to sing
Knew somehow that beside the Avon's flood
Fine stone lay ready for the quarrying.

Where he had thrown his glove, a church arose,
Built without mortar, Roman fashion, tight;
Only a little chapel, but it soared;
The chief of its dimensions was the height.

Only a jewel-box; as Bradford grew,
The Normans built a towered church instead;
The tiny old basilica endured
Dishonor as a charnel for the dead.

Later, by turns, it was a granary,
A schoolroom, cottage; tenements were pressed
Around it, leaning on the stony face;
What they concealed, no scholar ever guessed . . .

Until a parson climbing on the hills
And gazing down beheld, a pebble's toss
From his own vicarage, a yellow roof,
A building shaped to symbolize the Cross.

Long had he sought foundations, ornaments
Carved by the saint, but never dared aspire
To find this miracle awaiting him—
The oldest English church preserved entire.

KING PHILIP FAR AWAY
Spain, 1598

Here, denuded of its hangings, is the little judgment hall
Where he sat, a lonely mortal with whole continents in
    thrall,
Men in galleons and gold-mines waiting only for his call.

On those heights they call *The Hermits*, every afternoon
    alone,
He would mount the *Chair of Philip*, watching from that
    granite throne,
Praying as his monastery grew gigantic, stone by stone.

When he was betrothed by proxy to a wife across the sea,
She was not much more a stranger to him than his other
    three,
Or than any human creature whom he sought would always
    be.

After people proved a burden ('Time is gold, which talk
    consumes),
All day long he wrote directions to ambassadors and
    grooms,
Council, gardeners, and subjects. Read the samples in his
    rooms!

Dying in this oratory, he could watch the candles' rays
Flicker through the church below him, faintly hear the
    chant of praise;
Soldiers winced to see his torment and his patience in
    those days.

43

LECTURE NEAR NOTTINGHAM
England: Byron's Tomb

Where collieries and farms are interknit,
En route to Hucknall, you have viewed the shabby
Cots of the miners, each a definite
Contrast to Byron's flower-gardened Abbey.
The Sexton spent his boyhood in the Pit,
But now for decades he has been a gabby
Guide to Avernus at the parish church,
Giving the benefit of his research.

His narrative, an aitch-less masterpiece,
Includes an agèd grandmother's descriptions
Of how His Lordship came embalmed from Greece
With an arrangement common for Egyptians
Laid in the pyramids: at obsequies
The heart and other notable exceptions
Followed the mummy in a little urn,
Walked by a mourner several yards astern.

The one word *Byron*, with his dates and wreath,
Adorns a panel like a manhole cover
Set in the floor to mark the vault beneath,
Where all his haughty relatives are over-
Looked (like the tomb-mates of Elizabeth),
Besides encountering a second bother:
The Byron family's coffins, neatly stacked,
Have telescoped as leaden sheets collapsed.

"Some queer professor, an American,
Doubted Milord was 'ere; so came an order

The vault be opened, and they made me stand
Close as I am to you while some reporter
Looked at 'is foot; I patted Byron's 'and;
You'd know 'im, though 'e's shrunk eight inches
        shorter."
The Sexton's farewell clasp is putting you in
Touch with the quill that scribbled off *Don Juan.*

THE LEPER WINDOW
England: Stoke Poges

Unheeded, crouching by the lowermost
Panes, you could view the crucifix on high
And turn your mutilations toward the Host;
Even discard your rattle, let it lie.

Prayers may redeem the wretched who have sinned,
Wherefore men cut this window in the stones;
Kneeling inside they worshipped while the wind
Snapped like a cur at your tormented bones.

Here, unobtrusive, you partook of Bread
Among the graves—the cleanly, sheltered dead.

LINES COMMENDING SELF-DECEPTION
211 Sproul Hall, Davis

Defying winter and your finer feelings
With plastic violets, I fill a vase;
Imperious as March, I flaunt the iris
I have kept hidden in the filing case.

A connoisseur appreciates illusion,
Prefers the golden mirror to the true,
Seeks after love's delectable confusion,
And grows immortal with a glass or two.

So let my peach twigs flower in the office,
My pulses flutter with imagined spring,
And let no bee's unnecessary logic
Disturb the hum of air-conditioning.

LINES IN PRAISE OF MENTAL LAPSES

Illogic plays its tricks on me
With unpredictability.
Cartographers may sweat in vain
To show a definite terrain;
Though signposts herald the Grand Canyon
And we have traveled that way often,
The road was different, I recall—
Those pines should not be there at all—
And inwardly a childish tone
Maintains, "It's more like Yellowstone."

Need mental cogs be always meshing?
Their little lapses are refreshing.
When I review an ancient story,
The author, if he knew, would glory:
Though seven times his book I've read,
I still am easily misled.
Tom Jones' behavior seems so shady,
I panic lest he lose his lady;
Beholding Juliet in bloom,
I'm certain she'll escape the tomb.

Illogicality's a curse,
But mine's a lively universe.

LOST POEMS

Caesar escaped with his Commentaries,
Swimming the sidestroke and holding them high,
But some books of the *Queen of Faeries*
Burned when those rascals made Spenser fly;
One Betsy Baker, to line each pie,
Greased rare comedies (God forgive her),
Paper then being in short supply.
Tales like these make a poet shiver.

Sloppy scribes were the adversaries
Tormenting Chaucer, until they nigh
Ruined his works, gave him coronaries;
Coleridge, starting to versify
Kubla Khan, let some passer-by
Dam the flow of his *sacred river*,
And later found it had all gone dry.
Tales like these make a poet shiver.

Buried away in those mortuaries
Where ancient volumes, envellumed, lie,
Handled only by antiquaries,
With pages uncut—and you soon see why—
There are countless lyrics that did not die,
Having been stillborn, or kept in their quiver
Like ill-made arrows with shafts awry.
Tales like these make a poet shiver.

MEDITATIONS ON GRIEF
Kenilworth Castle

Handsome Lord Leicester lies
Haggard and sleeping,
Effigy on a tomb,
With no one weeping.

Five hundred years were blown
High with his castle;
His moat is stopped with earth;
So is the tattle.

Kenilworth, insolent
Dower of queens,
Which were the dungeons here,
Which the latrines?

This afternoon a child,
Viewing these fables,
Played with a tiny toad
Found near the stables.

Gusts blew it from her hand
Off the Strong Tower;
When she beheld it dead,
Tears fell, a shower.

MICHELANGELO'S "DAY"
Florence

The titan surges from his resting-place
Detailed in limbs and trunk, each muscle taut,
But shocks us with the fragment of a face,

As if the hand that painted God could not
Chisel the glaring countenance of Day
Or, shuddering, destroyed what it had wrought.

Here is no Grecian legacy, the prey
Of buried ages; nor the residue
After fanatics hammered art away:

But as blind Oedipus must grieve anew
At dawn and feel his bed a winding-sheet,
The weary sculptor, driven to pursue

His toil, at last awakened to defeat
Confronting Day and left this incomplete.

51

MINOR MEDICI

In carving one of his statues for the Medici tombs at Florence, Michelangelo idealized beyond recognition the features of Lorenzo, usurping Duke of Urbino, an unworthy grandson of Lorenzo the Magnificent.

Florence degraded and himself enslaved,
The sculptor carved this tomb for Vanity,
This monument to hide a rubbish heap.
But as he labored, disillusioned, ill,
The art that lifted David's head so high
And liberated Moses from the rock
Transformed a weak usurper to a god.

In this calm chapel where Magnificence,
His forebear, lies unmarked beneath a slab,
Unworthy young Lorenzo, purified,
Sits with a helmet shadowing his grief,
Athena's knight and her philosopher.
Those fingers, pressing silence like a chord,
Would not have snatched Urbino's ducal crown;
Such noble loins never begot that queen
Who massacred ten thousand innocents.

"Let us forget," said Michelangelo,
"How we beheld him—greedy, arrogant,
Polluting all his comeliness and power.
He is transfigured, moving out of Time,
And I portray him as he may be now,
In anguish for his country and his soul."

MOMENT AT RAVENNA
Italy: Tomb of Galla Placidia

The old brick casing of the tomb appalls
The traveller—until he steps within.
As through an eyelid, there the sunshine falls
Reddened through little windowpanes of thin
Translucent alabaster. Suddenly
All the mosaics of the dome awake;
The chapel blossoms with a galaxy:
Stars in the bluest heaven, a blazing crown;
Doves, martyrs, emblematic harts who slake
Their longing where the water rushes down.

How near the builders were to Galilee,
Nearer than I can journey! By the dim
Sarcophagus with glory overhead
I mourn that blessed interlude, too brief,
When saints were comforted by seraphim,
And the most halting traveller was led
By young religion, and a strong belief.

MORE STATELY MANSIONS

The kings of Portugal, though less
Pearly than nautili,
Would slough their outgrown palaces
For grander ones nearby;
Their pseudocastles on the crags
Still flabbergast the eye.

When Ferdinand and Isabel
Ousted the royal Moor,
On his mosaicked Alcazar
They built an upper floor;
Their heels clicked high above the halls
He'd gloried in before.

At Hampton Court, where pensioners
Now hoist their bread on ropes,
King Henry, like a hermit crab
Usurping Wolsey's hopes,
Appropriated to himself
A dwelling fit for popes.

In Venice, like a millionaire's
Discarded Cadillac,
Palazzos pass to hoi polloi;
Americans may track
Through chambers where Lord Byron sinned
Or Marco Polo packed.

MURGATROYD

1001 D Street, Davis

Whenever we would open, there he stood,
With the supreme authority of need:
The face with pansy markings, eyes alight;
The body young, as meager as a bird's
Under the lusterless neglected fur.

Our cat confronted him, the Amazon,
Disdainful princess, nourished and secure,
Swinging her paw at the intruder there;
He quivered, but continued hovering
As if it were impossible to fail.

Our guilt, intolerable, weighed us down:
After three days, a saucerful of milk;
Complete capitulation, gates ajar
To grooming and a cushion and our love.
These were his right; he never questioned it.

NEAR AN ENGLISH CATHEDRAL

At Winchester the yellow leaves were warm
Above the churchyard where we strolled an hour;
The great medieval wall went journeying
Past us, an altitude without a tower.

John Keats on a September afternoon
Loved the cathedral and the crickets' song,
The stubble, warmer than the fields of spring—
Lamenting that he would not be there long.

Two years before, Jane Austen came, who wrote
Of the *declining year*, the *tawny* bough,
And blessèd *images of youth and hope*;
Her name is there in the cathedral now.

NEAR THE PENOBSCOT
Maine

Past lilac and past currant bush in back,
Along a pitchy footpath set with shells,
And through the door bescratched by paws of Jack
You walked into the kitchen with its smells:
The coffee grinder, pork-and-beans of Maine,
Indian pudding, brandied deermeat pies,
The fragrance from the shelf where Cousin Jane
Had set the dough in yeasty pans to rise.

There was her alcove with the plants in bloom,
Her window where a child could scan the sights
Of Elm Street from a rocker and consume
Giant dill pickles with the *Arabian Nights*.
    Gingerbread castle—architect's despair—
    But how you wish it still were standing there!

NEW ENGLAND RENEWAL
Old Sturbridge, Massachusetts

If homestead means security and roots,
The moving of a house may seem profane,
A portent joggling along the road
Like Birnam Wood en route to Dunsinane.

These migrant buildings, though, were refugees
Needing asylum of a proper sort,
Like holy grottos flying overseas
Or monasteries crated for export.

This village had an ancient meeting-house,
Schoolrooms, a tavern to revivify,
Not settings that a landscape painter built
For silken-skirted milkmaids at Versailles.

Suspended life resumes, dips candle-wax,
Grinds wheat by water, hammers out a nail,
And drives its wagon through the covered bridge,
Like sleepers set agoing in a tale.

Seeking my own renewal, I have come
To break such bread, finger a knubby yarn,
And drink again the atavistic scent
Of timothy and horses in a barn.

NEXT OF KIN
Pasadena, California

How imperceptibly the smog has come
Between the sunlight and this wooden porch
Where Grace, my cousin, loved to talk with me:
My smarting vision cannot reach the slopes
Of mountains, my security in youth,
Nor the observatory high above
That faithfully reminded men of stars;
Our city might be on a prairie now,
With no horizon but this horrid haze.

I have come back unheralded today,
Seeking that elder cousin who was kind.
Her name, the telephone I knew by heart,
Have disappeared from the directory;
And as I sped along through hazy streets,
My recollections faltered, out of date
Like the addresses from my girlish years.
I found her house behind a newer one,
But on the threshold a young woman said:
"She died at Christmas; we have bought the place."

Oh, frail, contemptible my loyalty;
My heart is narrow—I confess it now.
Her love endured after I moved away,
But I, preoccupied with fresh concerns,
Skimmed through her letters and postponed reply.
She baked for me and knitted me a scarf,
Observed my birthday—hers I never knew.
Last winter suddenly she wrote no more,

And I supposed her angry; messages
To her seemed posted down a hollow tree,
And no one told me she had fallen ill.

Incredulous of changes as a child,
I still resolved to visit her at last,
Making all good with presents and a feast;
Now here's the house, with strangers at the door
I used to open freely as my own.

Her love persisted, but her quiet joy
In me was overshadowed long ago
By unresponsiveness, like flowers grown
Behind this dark, intolerable smog.

NORTHERN WATERFALL
Canada

Close to the brink we tremble and discard
Language; the miracle that we espy
Deep in the forest needs no human cry;
This lonely cataract shall still bombard,
Centuries after we are gone, the scarred
Ledges and echo in the northern sky.
What can our coming hither signify,
Our veneration, or our disregard?

Life is dispensed in drops, and here the scale
Seems overgenerous: though mind would keep
Majesty in remembrance, ear shall fail
To resonate the thunder it has known,
Eye to recall this water, like the sweep
Of an immortal's garment from his throne.

NOT AS ORDERED

A shy but golden little love I prayed,
Slipping demurely underneath my dress,
Warm as a heart-shaped locket to caress
My meditations; and the wish you made
Implored a tiny pleasure-skiff arrayed
For swishing round the swanlake—lilies, yes,
Or kisses gathered softly without stress
Until the parting on the esplanade.

Never in all my fantasies I sought
These glowing rubies that bemuse the brain
Of every yokel, making care a lodger
Within my breast; and you are all untaught
To steer this galleon full rigged for Spain
And flaunting rakishly the Jolly Roger.

ON A FRIEND'S ACHIEVEMENT

She has been patient as those Tyrian
Women who toiled for hours in the surf
To win a robe of triumph: standing there
With ocean foaming cold about their knees,
They pulled the somber threads that they had spun
Through seashells, ever drawing forth a dye,
A royal purple, from the life within.

ON A LARGER SCALE

The planets have their tragedies: where Mars
Fronts Jupiter, the night remains unpearled;
That solemn interval between two stars
Records the dissolution of a world.
Pluto, though once a loyal satellite,
Is now dissevered from his master sphere;
Earth's lonely kinsman, farthest from the light,
He traces an interminable year.

And stars may love: Polaris circles round
The partner of his great impassioned dance—
A secret happiness, for she is drowned,
Incorporated in his radiance.
    Men still repeat what galaxies portray
    In dramas older than the Milky Way.

ON A WAY OF KEEPING RECORDS
Pasadena, California

As they forewarned me, I have found
Only a hollow in the ground
To show that my father's house stood there
With a wooden tower that cleft the air,
And a broad veranda halfway round.

If earth holds on to a cellar, why
Does the space above it forget, deny
What stood for decades, a friendly sight
Toward which the linnets would bend their flight?
Indifferent void that we occupy!

But wait, these are markers: the myrtle's bloom
Now points exactly to where my room
Awoke by a bower of pink one day;
The jacaranda, a vast bouquet,
Had reached the turret that final June.

ONE LIFE TOO SHORT

"One life too short, my woman's heart too small,"
You say, "to be the vessel of love's grace."
Yet when the primal earth became annealed,
Less was the miracle than when the heart
Was firmed and molded to encompass love.
Planets in their eternal harmony
Glide with no larger liberty or scope
Than love along the pathway it has traced.

You have not entered such a universe
Before; a new dimension is revealed.
Every familiar landmark disappears,
The ancient highroads are obliterate,
And worthless all the worn and ragged maps
Inked by our ancestors. Forgetting these,
Prepare the vessel now, sustained by love
And strong with an immortal surety:
Move in the radiance from which a spark
Was borrowed for man's breath, the amplitude
Of life, and the infinity of heart.

ON THE DIKE
Volendam

Safe on the island, sheltered by the dike,
A cow is grazing with a ray of sun
Touching her side, a sight so comforting
You fancy how a milkmaid's forehead leans
There for a moment, and recall the spurt
Warm from the udder, milk in sportiveness
Aimed at the mouth of a delighted child.

The dike's a hillock velvety with grass,
Not like a barrier; you scramble up,
Still boy enough to wish that you might roll,
But eager also to attain the view.
Once at the summit, you stand shivering.

Beyond lies nothing but the northern sea,
Hungry, forbidding, infinite as death;
Beyond the dike a wilderness of waves
No majesty, but cold monotonous
Miles of gray water ruffled by the wind.

ON THE UNDERGROUND
London

Chaucer and Raleigh more
Here than upon the floor
Of London at our door
   Radiate power.
Tunneling past we scan
Antediluvian
Names—subterranean
   Aldgate, the Tower.

Here Donne's reliques are blent;
The human continent
Diminished when he went;
   This he enlarges.
Dust of his lady's hair
Shines in the earth somewhere;
Atoms like those must bear
   Positive charges.

Here most the buried homes,
Taverns, cathedral domes,
The vitalizing bones,
   Quicken our wonder;
Bombings cannot destroy
The elemental joy
Hidden as deep as Troy
   Nine cities under.

THE PARSON'S WIFE

Surely He meant me to live circumspectly,
Stepping at farthest to the garden shed
To tend a lamb with moist umbilic thread
And wrinkled fleece; always to bob abjectly
Under a cottage lintel; move correctly
My cautious fingertips on table spread
With willow cups, and nod judicious head
While other rural ladies chat sedately.

He did not mould this body to embrace
A demigod, these useful hands to be
Rumpling informally the atrocious grace
Of panthers dozing, nor this soul to flee
Singing through interplanetary space.
Will He be angry? Will He punish me?

THE PHOENIX NEST
Goethe's Birthplace, Frankfurt am Main

Bombers destroyed his boyhood home and left
    Hardly a sliver, yet the whole is there;
Builders evoked that unforgotten shape
    Like ectoplasm mounting through the air.

Cellar to gable, this is what he saw:
    Glass of the kind that human lungs have blown,
Nails wrought by hand and hammered in the floor
    Just where the faithful photograph has shown.

Back from their exile come the writing desk,
    The stove with colored pictures of the Flood,
The chapbooks—one concerning Doctor Faust—
    The puppet show that turned to flesh and blood.

This man had power to renew himself,
    Ever revitalized by lyric speech;
When loves had shaken him like cannon blasts,
    He rallied and composed a book on each.

Out of the ashes of himself he rose
    Many a time more philosophic, free;
He never tasted death, but closed his eyes,
    Slept like a conqueror at eighty-three.

POSTSCRIPT
San Francisco

Somehow I'd very much prefer,
Angry and severed though we stand,
You wouldn't play our games with her.

In darkness of the theater,
No message folded in her hand,
Somehow I'd very much prefer.

At midnight when the treetops stir
Around our wall in lotus land,
You wouldn't play our games with her?

That no one turn astronomer,
Nestled up there where views expand,
Somehow I'd very much prefer.

And promise if someday she were
To want the little house we planned,
You wouldn't play our games with her.

Though you're exasperating, sir,
And love henceforth is contraband,
Somehow I'd very much prefer
You wouldn't play our games with her.

PREDICTION
Capitol Park, Sacramento

Sit where you are upon the grass and raise
Your eyes to portents in the clouds above me,
And let me read in that translucent gaze
What miracles must follow when you love me.
I shall upset the universal order,
Tasting more rapture than the rules allow,
And overskip the consecrated border
Of mediocrity that hems me now.

With such a lever, I can move creation;
Glowing with double courage I shall dare
Topple dictatorships and ease our nation
Of all the grievances it groans to bear.
    I cannot yet announce when this will be;
    Your eyes on April clouds are baffling me.

PROPHETS

Beside my walk the thunderstricken pine
Sullies the woodland with its blackened trunk,
And white cliffs blasted by the powder-mine
Brood over waters where their top has sunk.
The harvester moves on across the field,
Finality rotating in the sun,
Leaving the stubble and the clods unhealed
Where golden ripples of the wheat have run.

Here long ago the river burst its gates
And plunging seaward with triumphant roar
Left pools to stagnate in the canyon straits
Where the unfathomed depths had gleamed before.
　　These! Yet until today I never knew
　　The barrenness of life despoiled of you.

RARITIES

Moosehead Lake, Maine

Back where geraniums are grown in pots
My mother's rosebush flowered every year;
We children eyed it, but we never plucked
The only roses we had come so near.

Where birches trembled high above the lake
A random cherry tree had taken root;
We climbed it daily till the crop was ripe,
A scant half-dozen of the tiny fruit.

And when the steamboat *Kineo* tied up,
We hungered for the cookies, rich with spice,
That Captain Hiram treasured in a can;
He shared them once a year or maybe twice.

SAMPLES

I sampled only tiny bits of you,
  And from the salvage who surmises whether
I minded that your regiment withdrew
  After we'd danced a time or so together?

The doodled program from the symphony,
  The four-leaf clover and the periwinkle,
The goodbye letter whose philosophy
  Ends in a sudden caper and a twinkle!

Some hoard a pebble found near Parthenon,
  A pumice fetched from Krakatao's crater;
Trifles are oftentimes the colophon
  Not to a small adventure, but a greater.

SEMANTICS

I

Meeting your eyes today, I wished that all
Spoke to me thus, for language only blurs
The illumination that a look confers;
Discoursing, men are aliens in thrall.
Like convicts we may tap upon the wall
That separates our living sepulchers;
With twitching ropes for our interpreters,
Like divers, wordless, through the deep we call.

Terror goes vaguely guessed, like some forlorn
Entreaty cut upon a windowpane
By an imprisoned queen, or bottle-borne
Over the choking surges all in vain.
Urgent our message, but the wings are torn,
Entangled woefully within a skein.

II

I am a shaggy savage in a cave,
Daubing by torchlight a similitude;
Like a barbaric poet, in my rude
Tongue would express divinity and save
Scripture; a schoolboy, finding in its grave
One stony vertebra, would thence conclude
How to rebuild the behemoth, or brood
Over Leviathan's primeval wave.

You smile, envisioning the awkward hand
Or tongue or brain unequal to such art,
Harmony, science; but today I stand
Helpless as my forefathers to impart
A simple thought through language or expand
My universe to reach another's heart.

III

Before the world began for us, I lay
Cradled between my mother's sides, more near
Than breathing, yet her happiness and fear
Remote; the arteries that now convey
Food to my isolation, the array
Of cells, are sullen servitors who hear
Coldly my words, tomorrow mutineer
Against their master, and at length decay.

Divided are the units that comprise
Man and his kingdom; if we rebels plot
Union, the insufficiency and lies
Of language (our ambassador) allot
A separation; though the lover dies
In the belovéd's arms, he knows her not.

THE SHOWPIECE
Maine, 1912

Though David nearly labored his young heart out
Clearing the farm of rocks, which he would range
Neatly in walls, one boulder was accepted
As something in his life he could not change.

It towered and he had to plow around it,
The main frustration in his world of stone,
Like a titanic missile from Katahdin;
The glacier must have dropped it with a groan.

Seeing this giant proof against his pebbles,
David discreetly laid the sling aside,
Had himself photographed upon the boulder
Holding a son and bristling with pride.

SKULL CAVE
Lava Beds National Monument

Lingering there with lava all around,
He grew insistent and articulate.
We studied out the Indian battleground,
The rocky strongholds, trench, of long ago;
And sweated to recall the molten hate,
The rage and malice he himself had found,
All rigid now as the volcanic flow.

He talked, and I endured his chronicle,
My retina bedeviled by the glare,
The silver tears and flashes in the air;
His eyes confronting the irreparable.

After we reached the cavern, he prevailed:
I dangled with him from the ribby, stern
Downdrop of iron. Here a pictograph
Ochered the wall—moons, arrows, men impaled—
A hieroglyphic I could not discern,
Although he pointed with a bitter laugh.

Interpreting, he led me where the east
Vanished, and deeper in the catacomb
Twilight revealed the rib-cage of a beast
Under a skully curvature, the dome.

He knew the sequence and ignored my fear,
Pressing through labyrinths of his own choice,
Curves like the convolutions of an ear
Reverberating to that endless voice . . .

Till almost slipping, frost upon our breath,
We neared a frozen pool among the stones,
Lusterless and unchanging, like a death;
As icy as the pit where Judas groans
By solid rock, the blindness of despair.
Turning, he waited for my verdict there.

STATE OF PRESERVATION
Britain

When Cromwell "slighted" Kenilworth,
The chapels, being shoddy, fell;
He bared the kitchens deep in earth
And left the banquet-hall a shell.

Only a graceful window-sheath
Recalls how Leicester loved to take
His wine with great Elizabeth;
The castle's cut like wedding-cake.

Far to the north at Linlithgow
The palace floors are winterworn,
The naked hearths are piled with snow,
Where once a royal girl was born.

Powder and vengefulness prevail,
And yet at Warwick I have seen
A handkerchief, at Wilton pale
Hair that belonged to England's queen.

Fire and time relentlessly
Burn, yet at Holyrood I found
A basket for embroidery—
The silken skeins that Mary wound.

TIMELY TRANSLATION
Andersen's "Tinderbox"

The soldier's eyes were boyish, round with wonder
In the enchanted hollow of that tree:
There lay the treasure as the witch had promised,
Coppers, but comforting to poverty.

Now blessings on her, though egad how ugly!
When I mistrusted her, I little knew:
She has endowed me with a tavern fire,
Dinner, a bottle for my comrades too.

Greater fulfillment, chests of gold and silver!
He showered pennies on the cavern floor,
Reburdening his pockets and his knapsack
Till boots could barely shuffle through the door.

Now I can buy a windmill or a dairy,
A fleet of vessels trading far from home.
His eyes grew narrow as the riches mounted:
I may achieve the princess and her throne.

But presently the venom of a serpent
Flowed into him, the ugly hag's command:
Surprise your foemen, burn, lest they destroy you;
A helpful instrument is at your hand.

He clutched as if he saw a jewel coffer;
Threw off his money, clambered up the rope,
And staggered from the barren tree with nothing
Except the tinderbox, that evil hope.

TOKEN

You ask a sign.
Beloved infidel, would sibylline
Pronouncements make me worthy in your sight?
Rod squirming into snake, sword wrenched from stone,
Blue incandescence round my head at night
Work your conversion? Or must Odin's lone
Eye reassure you, since of the divine
        You ask a sign?

        A sure behest
You would require, injunction manifest.
The fig branch that shall never fructify,
The thicket unconsumed where flames are hot,
In This Sign Conquer scrolled across the sky:
We lack such glaring portents, but is not
The voice that speaks like God within my breast
        A sure behest?

"TO PLUCK BRIGHT HONOUR"
Yorkshire

Before his wounds defrauded
Lord Percy of his breath,
Like his great kinsman Hotspur
He had marshalled hosts to death.

Awe-stricken by such glory,
A knight said, "Let him lie
Enshrined in Fountains Abbey
While human time goes by."

Now travelers must shiver
To see a downpour search
The noseless, blackened image
There in the roofless church.

Few study the inscription,
Late-written and obscure:
This may have been a Percy;
We cannot tell for sure.

TRICHO-NYMPHA

The termite tapping underneath
Is seeking wood he may devour,
And yet himself cannot digest
My kitchen flooring, turned to flour.
Fermenting it, he needs the sly
Assistance of a firm ally.

Unlike a youth whose diamond lens
Beholds a nymph in drops of dew,
The famous Joseph Leidy once
Studied a termite through and through—
A gut like freeways when they vex us,
As crowded as corrals in Texas.

The protozoans herded there
Are swollen, bell-shaped; and the goody
They manufacture for their host
Is pickle-juice, no longer woody.
All hail to such cooperation,
Which antedates the human nation!

Our scholarly anatomist,
Although Victorian, had seen
Burlesque; and since those flagellates
Recalled a many-streamered queen
Whose dancing gladdened him somehow,
Their name is Tricho-nympha now.

TWO O'CLOCK FEEDING
Davis, California, 1943

Waking . . . and he and I are still alone,
This baby overyoung to look or smile;
Out in the stormy garden, branches moan,
But here the yellow lamplight beams awhile.
There is a comfort in my room, the sound
Of gentle sucking, and the touch of joy,
As carefully I fold a blanket round
The frailness of this downy newborn boy.

Be grateful, heart, seeing that here at least
He may lie warm and know his mother's voice;
Seeing that hungry little lips may feast
With dimples round the nipple. Oh, rejoice,
   Since for an hour he is guarded here,
   Nestled and warmed and nurtured, safe from fear.

TWO PAIRS OF GLOVES
Elizabeth I and Charlotte Brontë

Two pairs of gloves in a glassy case:
The tiny ones are commonplace,
Well worn besides and mended well;
But these, long-fingered, nonpareil,
Adorned a queen for a little space.

Two separate ways the ladies went;
Their hearts were not so different:
What hammerings their gloves have masked
When veins rebellious, overtasked,
Admitted no impediment.

UNDER THE BELL JAR

Burns's Last Home, Dumfries, Scotland

His poems taxidermized under glass
　　Like wild birds that have ceased to utter cries—
A parlor group with wire viscera,
　　And cotton in their throats, and beads for eyes.

Upstairs the signature on bedroom pane
　　(Incised with what?—he had no diamond tool)
Protected by another sheet of glass
　　From vandals or the fingerpressing fool.

And near the church, where all the headstones grow
　　Gigantic as if nourished by his loam,
We find a sculptured Muse and ploughboy kept
　　Immaculate beneath a crystal dome.

Before they set him in the showcase there,
　　He had a grassy corner out of view,
And never having been a marble man,
　　He would be homesick for it if he knew.

THE UNFINISHED WINDOW

To prove how rare a palace he had wrought,
Aladdin left a single casement plain,
Not jeweled like the others, and besought
The Emperor to finish the design.

Though slaves came bearing basins full of gems,
And artists labored for their lord's delight,
Never in years of industry could men
Match what the genie had devised one night.

Confronting magic, craftsmanship must fail—
As if a well-intentioned artisan
Told Chaucer how to end the Squire's Tale,
Gave Coleridge some hints for *Kubla Khan*.

THE UNLOVED LADIES

Oh, surely Leah's mind misgave
    When, harassed by her father's pleas,
She veiled her reddened eyes to brave
    The thousand infelicities
    Of earthen water pitcher squeezed
Between two brazen bowls. What art
    Can burnish their biographies,
The ladies doomed to half a heart?

When Tristram fled across the wave
    Despairing at the flippancies
Of Irish queen but still her slave,
    Another young Isolt gave ease
    Awhile and won his gallantries
Because her name was counterpart;
    But they can only drink the lees,
The ladies doomed to half a heart.

So Mary Lincoln strove to save
    Her husband from his agonies
Outrivaled by a prairie grave;
    Forgive her craze for luxuries,
    Nor listen to her blasphemies,
For all their lives are full of smart
    And lonely are their obsequies,
The ladies doomed to half a heart.

    Madam, from such analogies
Who would compile herself a chart?
    Never I thought to rank with these,
The ladies doomed to half a heart.

A VICTORIAN CASTLE
Penrhyn, Wales

The mind mistrusts perfection: when you saw
Those towers notching heaven without a flaw—
The barbican, the drawbridge, the immense
Donjon—you doubted them despite your awe.

A modern fairytale, says common sense;
Never a sword was drawn in its defense;
Tempest and time have not begun to gnaw
The candied sleekness of those battlements.

Here is a huge hypocrisy of stone,
A falsehood it were futile to excuse,
Cemented with Jamaicans' blood and bone;
Levered in place by the exhausted thews
Of tenantry and miners, Britain's own;
Here stands a monument to parvenus.

VISITATION

You came when no one saw you, long ago;
I dreamt myself a lady in brocade
Whom a rich earl embraced incognito
By torchlight in a bower he had made.
You were a poet strayed from town to meet
A pastor's daughter with a country air;
You offered songs, incomparably sweet,
And kissed the flaxen plaitings of my hair.

Godlike you came, a swan, a flood of gold
To overwhelm adoring womankind;
I must not light my taper, overbold
To view your beauty, lest it strike me blind.
   I was the more deceived, my lord, in you,
   But it was long ago and no one knew.

VISIT TO A YOUNG WIFE

I neither envy nor begrudge your bliss
Now a capricious destiny unlocks
For you the gateway that withstood my shocks
So many years; I take it not amiss,
Telling myself if I am Beatrice
Some other must attend to Dante's socks;
The one familiar prickly paradox
That chafes my magnanimity is this:

You are so rich in him, you often read
Instead of gazing when you have him here;
And sometimes pay his kisses little heed,
Yet part from him without a thrust of fear,
Knowing he will return to you—indeed
The thought of this can touch me very near.

WHERE ARE THEY NOW?

Hexham Abbey, England

What was the name of that would-be Caesar,
Once engraven upon your stone,
Or his brother, who murdered him
And erased it to rule alone?
Where is the Saxon who made your plaster
Mixed with ox-blood, as hard as bone?

Far to seek are the bishop saints,
Ornaments of your sacred chair,
And the great Northumbrian warrior-kings
Whom they blest and anointed there—
Fugitive as that wretch who sought
Sanctuary in his despair.

Nevermore will the monks descend,
Midnight feet that have worn your tread;
Now the staircase, though climbing still,
Leads to nothing, overhead.
What became of the Scots who fired
The rooftree, shedding these drops of lead?

Gone like snow; but I need not ask
After some you have sculptured there:
Gluttony with his honey-cakes,
Pride a-prinking her precious hair,
And the fox who harangues the geese;
These survive and are not too rare.

ZONE OF SILENCE
Ravenna

Tides of the midland sea no longer fret
These pebbles, for the harbor has gone dry
Like an old heart that once was passionate.
Dante, in pinewood paradise nearby,
Prayed to be free of his revengefulness
And saw his lady, a divine reply.

City of Dusk that sheltered his distress,
Ravenna holds a plaza where no more
Horn shall resound or busy wheel oppress.
Men hush their voices when they stand before
That temple where the carven laurels are—
Those Latin words proclaiming at the door
The poet's sepulchre. Within, a star,
A small red light, is burning up above
To mark the presence of enduring love.